# POMME & GRANITE

dear M

he line of blue is yellow

a wet line

the scent of black is an eye

or sand

th alculus of tou 's red

in error

the touch of s lue

is a taste

S

# POMME & GRANITE

SARAH RIGGS

1913 PRESS

PUBLISHED BY 1913 PRESS

JOURNAL1913.ORG



ISBN 978-0-9906332-0-4

1913 BOOKS ARE DISTRIBUTED BY

SMALL PRESS DISTRIBUTION

WWW.SPDBOOKS.ORG

PRINTED ON ACID-FREE, RECYCLED PAPER

IN THE UNITED STATES OF AMERICA

*for*

O

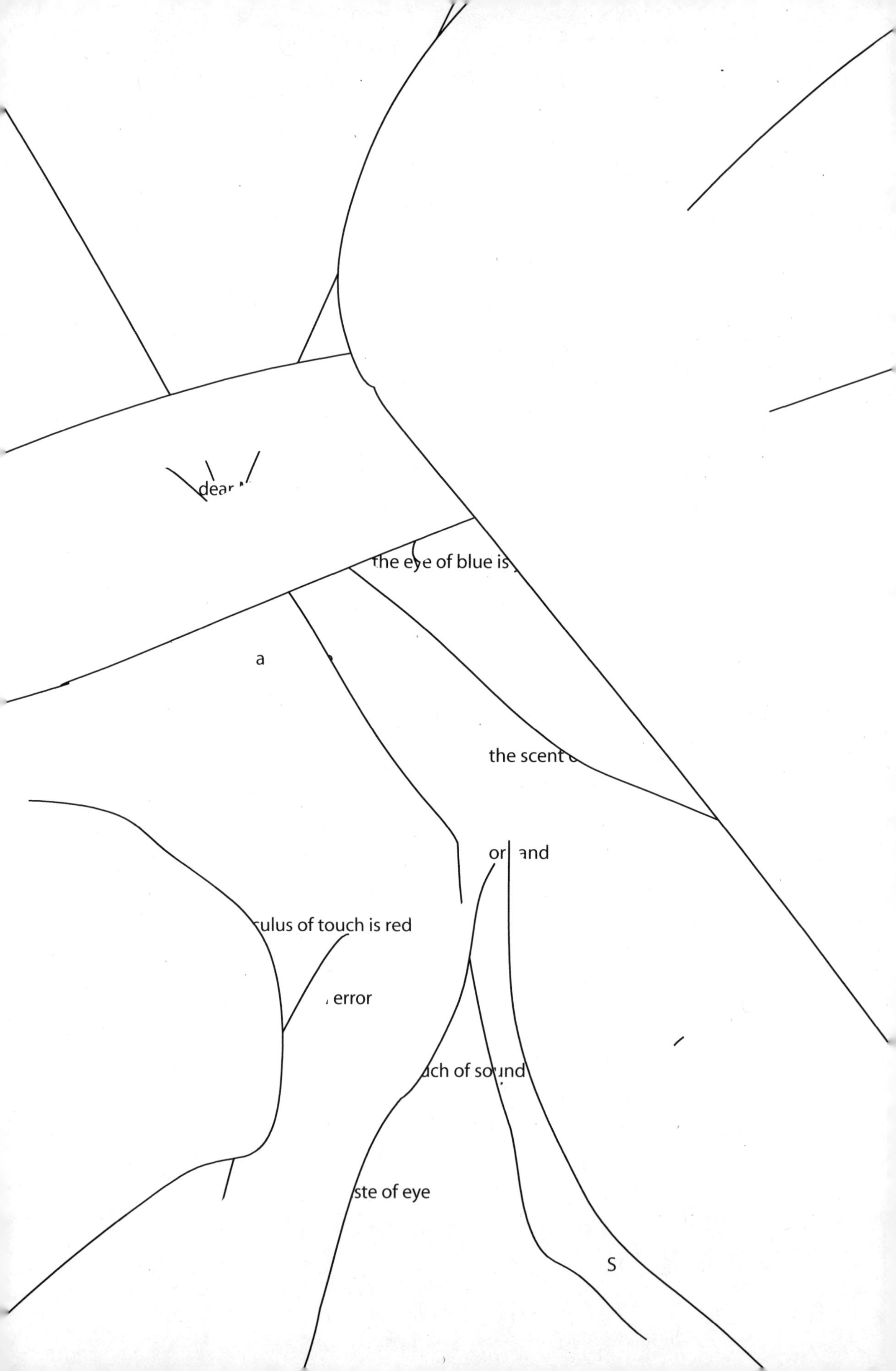

dear

the eye of blue is

a

the scent

or and

ulus of touch is red

error

ch of sound

ste of eye

s

# TOUCH, A BRIEF BOTANY

now with leaves the leaf layer
is open the underside touches
in those surfaces its veins
spread inward it is an outward
touching an inward the botanist
could explain to a point which
is a surface opening out composed
of many individual points
green but not sure
an unsure green all along
it's perhaps chartreuse

a surface composed whereas the under-
side is like skin that is lightly veined
that has veins like skin that has just
touched but who touches and who
receives the touching does touch begin
with the fingers the genitals or does it
begin surely that can be asked if touch
begins whether it has been happening all
along but less and less in the womb
all is touching nothing is not touching
a leaf is outside all that it is touching
itself the underside and above it is a maple
leaf fluttering from an absent tree abroad

the leaf is deeply present all along its
surface it is a maple a leaf intimately
known the maple it maples itself
touches broadly all along its veins
extends to its edges though the edges
are crisp would open out like the touch
of cheeks our cheeks touch and do not
touch our cheeks may touch sometime
the lack the two lacks may touch
the wish comes from a lack our cheeks
are drawn or puffed they touch the
touched cheeks the touch touches touch

touch won't deceive in a way in a way
we are used to it spreads through lies
till they dissolve or else language is a lie
in the presence of touch touch wouldn't
tell you this it is involved with that leaf
those cheeks it moves us as to what to
trust from this vantage you can see touch
or touch leaves based on trust on touch
some of it touch is a way of seeing
through of not seeing it's a leaf very
close-up too close to see touch has skin
and surface its leaves they open out

eye
calculus of touc
blue

# UNDERGROUND SONNETS

## WILL S.

Tell us, lines, what we should say. Let
the handwriting govern our movements.
Each key can lower the fingers gradually down.
Commentary goes rusty, awry. The house
must come clean. She sounds with garbled fields.
A seasonal grief she has, they say. But who
is she? The soup will be ready. Let us
hide out in the greasy parlance. A last
dash from germs. And none of it is ever
last, or lasting. We rein with these lines, bars
cross, disclose, open, our faces. There is
still one more line to fill, who is it for?
Dear, is it you, you reading, your line?

## WITHIN ARM'S REACH

My hand has reached out for you this many
semblance of mornings. If we were asked
why we were underground, how to answer?
As the fault of your sadness falls, these some
blossoms may need adjusting. Testing the
waters for our lungs, I find sticks in them,
whole branches veritably on leave—perhaps
why the poems root underground. "When the
sea hits those stones they talk." Occasionally
I love you more than the sky. How we
feel may tear this winter into spring and
if I don't say anything something happens.
But let me at least love you in the off-
season by phone. We shall love each other

*more than the elements, if I love you still more in the horizon*

## LOVE WINTER TOO

Dear Earth take in this fairy breath. Let it
seep into the mischievous crannies, the
rooks and rocks. What is behind the lily,
the foregone conclusion? If we look
at the interstices, the common lines
between sheets of rain. I wanted to write into
your heart but the chambers are closed. What
freedom in the rain when memory is for
sale? What response to give a fairy? We
manage, nonetheless, a raucous cheer
with the Daily Show, a tempestuous
cloud of letters. Even with pomegran-
ate molasses to soften the duck: we
cannot change, the most we can do is see.

*They dance the serrated edges of the leaves, the milky surface of the pond.*

# PHONE, PER SE

A conflict in the heart, or mind (*listen*).
And if you grew wings out of love for something
half-lost in you, note the phone calls you
back. Recall down there she really is queen.
A membrane of the earth opens here or
there, where there is bubbling & sulfur, the
girl drops down into a whole: becomes
a woman: (the hole) divides, the inter-
ior layers of skin are vibrant sheathes
(we can film them) not Alice this time she
no hare only pomegranate. Just this:
a ringing in the earth crust and no one
to pick up. A pause before the machine
begins to speak. And if we give the power away?

*Does a book bruise a body with snow?*

## SEQUENCE

Here are tidepools, some slate rock, a small
dead crab. The soft stones are red yellowish grey.
There's a rust orange unnameable
(hawkweed), oxeye, daisies, buttercup, white
iris, chives, meadow grass. "An ocean
of seaweed," snails spotted the size of
wide grains of sand, rockweed flung and spread,
waterbirds, barnacles on the rusted spheres
of the loading dock supports, some rock slime
walking on multiple small rocks to stay
the slippage, pigeons scattering from un-
derneath, a cinematic impression
of being under what's submerged at times,
being called back (knowing I would be)

*but by the mother's call: solitude at ease with attachment*

## LISTENING IN GRANITE MAJOR

And if this strange lady stands there frozen
like snow with the shadow garlands mingling
crinkled yellow and green, the beauty of
such marble that it softens the stoniness.
*She* Mother Nature, she is winter melting
spring both granite & grass are her domain,
her face white & green, there's no shade.
She warms the hills from that she does
not chase away herself, and turns them from
white to yes, she is stony because of
unyielding cruelty and he stonier still,
hard, harder still to think of her there picking
flowers in the grass—their color lost
from the herbs—not of a hill or a wall.

*The wind sits in the shoulder of your sail*

# DEAR WE,

To the short circle I have come alas
the winding gyre is not widening
but possibly whitening with my notebooks
which form hills, even small ridges, slate by
slate by Lake Champlain. My desire still
doesn't change its green, Exupéry's
baobab roots can be pulled out. And she
who is somersaulting, dancing in
her, who is finding her peace with her—
that smile, strength, says she is up
to the task. And what a slender fear when
the whole planet will be pulling out weeds.

*How gargantuan these weeds at the planet's edge*

## BREATHING SOME TIMES

Your voice a stream of words along my
imaginings. It's not quite the same through
the Reuben hips or dipping along the
protrusion of a Greek urn. Why Hades? He
too is part of the earth, just not the better
part. Only when we utterly accept winter
does spring become remotely possible.
When I come up for oxygen and you're
covering all the earth  (the pomegranate
splits open)  for awhile I need blackness
to feel myself breathing in and out.
Sometimes I miss you like wild down here.
From the interior you can see clearly
that the earth is, the earth is, not whole.

*And if the latent melodies circle into our breath.*

dear M

th

a w

the ca

ocean

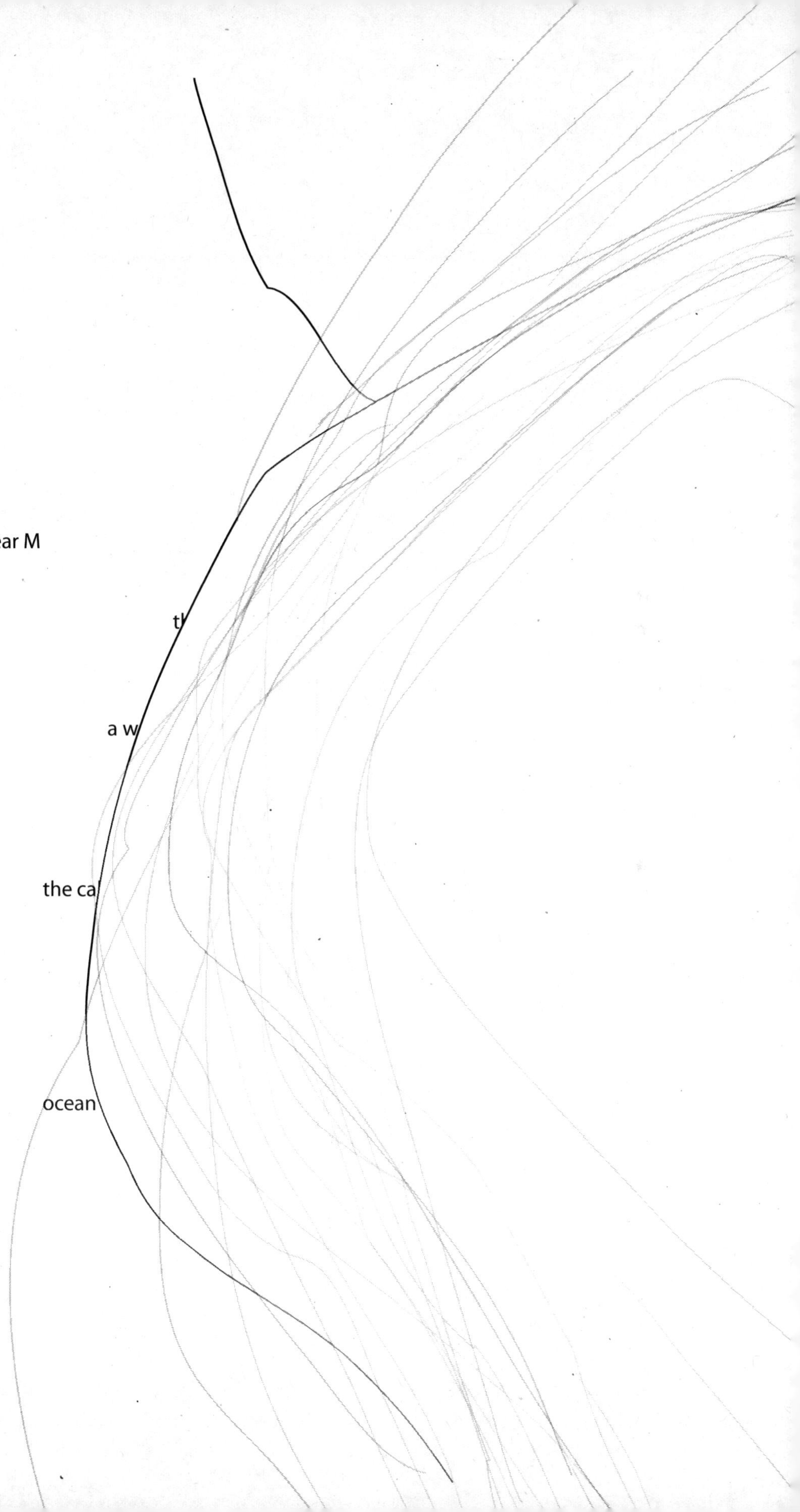

# RED TABLE

The phone calls you back
but down there she really is queen

the membrane of the earth opens
(where there is bubbling & sulfur)

the girl drops down into a whole (*the* hole)
becomes a woman: divided

the interior layers of skin
are colors and forms

(we can film them)

You open the book and each page is a

Mirror,
reflecting a strange face

Not you, & again not you
So many pages of not you

And this is what you use
What you cannot see or hear

Dear P,

Drop down under

Our sixth emotion is fear or sensuousness

Chance operations
We are grateful to sin

It providing so much of interest
fruitful developments

that continents divide, children are spawned, the underworld gets her queen, based on corporeal movements

can lust decide?

(and yet it was she who picked
the fruits

*And if you are the whole earth where are your offspring to go*

Women weave in and out of relief

I have nothing to say that has not

been enunciated in numerous languages

I am waiting for O through the thicket

of tourists of which we are part

At present there is not much to say

I'm at the early middle of something

that may well grow bigger than me.

*a long brass the size of a cheek*
*puffed out trumpets the sounds*
*the words would make*
*if fairies had speech*

This winter you inflict upon us is your morning. I saw a small cockroach in the metro, and thought momentarily we were in the Mission the verticality of those trees of love—
stop and     read their messages

the tearing of threads through the trees    thistle cap and wet: we race these valleys cyclic,
anemia, glass wear     it is Penelope who braids, flexes and it is in the undoing she stays
alive she undoes herself
the blunt tip of occasional grass is Pluto at large
there are three elements, almonds   and one of them is sleep

persistent roots & sulfur

A conflict in the heart, the mind (*listen:*

She peeled back,
let's say she tore

the yellow rind & picked out seven (six?)

pomegranate seeds

at each grain
her tongue twitched

a nymph was watching *someone always watching*

these few fleeting pleasures come with
heavy punishment (the west?)

Cinders of desire float in the Styx

*(Per prose) I want to write into the words*

the worlds the horizons the horizontals so long

the breath just a little further and so into the lungs

and if there are two one above and one below

we can gather all this oxygen though this alone may not be life

the modulation      breathe into these veins the veins

are turning blue (as the river Styx)

and the Harpies fly in with new passengers

some beaming bonus tickets a periodic metamorphosis

an almost-death or a giving life and then a return

the fluid tears and the erasures the fillings

the shifting of a book from one stack to another

to another the unfinished aspect of the mural

it is a wall become a window

the main was caught in you where the sulfur gapes

the sound as of a creaking door, but a baby, wakes the horizon

yet not recognizing it there in the balcony in the sun.

1 the mother draws the lines out as milk
2 the sonnets are hung in the window with care
3 our laundry has feet & this is a change
4 the feet swing in the breeze and the sock that's not missing laughs
5 and we had forgotten we are mammals?
6 entering the bee zone: ah ah ah  uh buzz buzz buzz
7 grotesque dreams of baby body parts
        in an inferno entryway
8 and we forget we are flesh?
9 the mother is very long
10 the baby monster wakes, her tongue comes first
11
12
13
14

the ripple of it: alive to possible
          shake    render    metamorphose

we animal
we close to the gods, to our own mortality
we can't make out

the feel of the darts
lets go the direct cushions

a more or less familiar
conversation drops into
background noise

we regret the brevity
of our journeys
but there are so many ways
to count home

these latent melodies
risk our generosity
we sink into the red velour

If we were to hold your orange

Across the traffic
(a little girl's tights)

1 fourteen lines of interruption to the sweltering rounds of fact
2 tossed in the mellifluous tilt of the egg beaters
3 in a carpaccio: fresh cold purple grapes. caravaggio.
4 who sleeps with abandon, hands frozen in relaxation
5 she dreams of the world she came from
        known to us only through our dreams of her dreams
6 the pink trim draws her into some sort of necessary net
7 weather reflects the human temperament, bouncing and jolting
8 as if at the rodeo, the iffy horses our own libido
9 trace the steps of the past with love of the present
for there is no other future
10 gently we strut these leaves en pleine ville
        full of our green
11 we shall have children all our lives & the daughter lets the mother go
12 this is how she comes and goes: the mother is strong
13 the ziffy bee whispers Arabic in the ear of the mother pollinated baby
14 normally she should have been born tomorrow, but what is normal?

across Rivoli just now our hundreds of nights together

            the sun shining through the January trees
            into my hair

February, the length of this month
           degrees of invasive procedure

violet ink
the shadows of branch
               and death goes up ^

## Demeter

leaves or none or few

do not drop in for an after-loss

pattern of all those
pass my verses

Your own glass shows you when you look in it

of hand,
of foot,
of lip,
of eye,
of brow

olives of endless age

Nebuchadnezzar can never know this ruin
We made        with our hands

Whether gentle or tumultuous
The horizons, at least, also uneven

We tapestry hot say as much
For the scarves
As they trail down the

Rest
Shread

the hierarchies in places
therever we are

the scarves are white lines
connecting the spirit world
with this one we know better

something falling

The diagonal verticality of the fairies

Sculpture of Eve naked and lavishly
seated with long ringlets of hair dropping
over and over an encurled serpent, very long,
overlaid & intermingled with ink leaves—

The Harpies flit in and out

the birded ones her friends

    their transformations out of fidelity
        to you

they grew wings out of love for something
    half-lost in you—

An Underworld defined by what it does not have—

though have you noticed
Paradise has next to none
of this either?

Lest sorrow lend                and words express

Love, yet, love        a thousand errors

Hate on                I engraft you new

To give away yourself keeps yourself still

*what about the look of the interstices,*
*the common lines between rain sheets?*

What's in the brain, that ink

Green my bad

Mine eye is in my mind

Million'd accidents creep in twixt vows

Tender inward

Will I swear beauty

Me from myself

Eye has taken

*I wanted to write into your heart*
*but the chambers seem closed.*
*The oceans are coming to wash us*

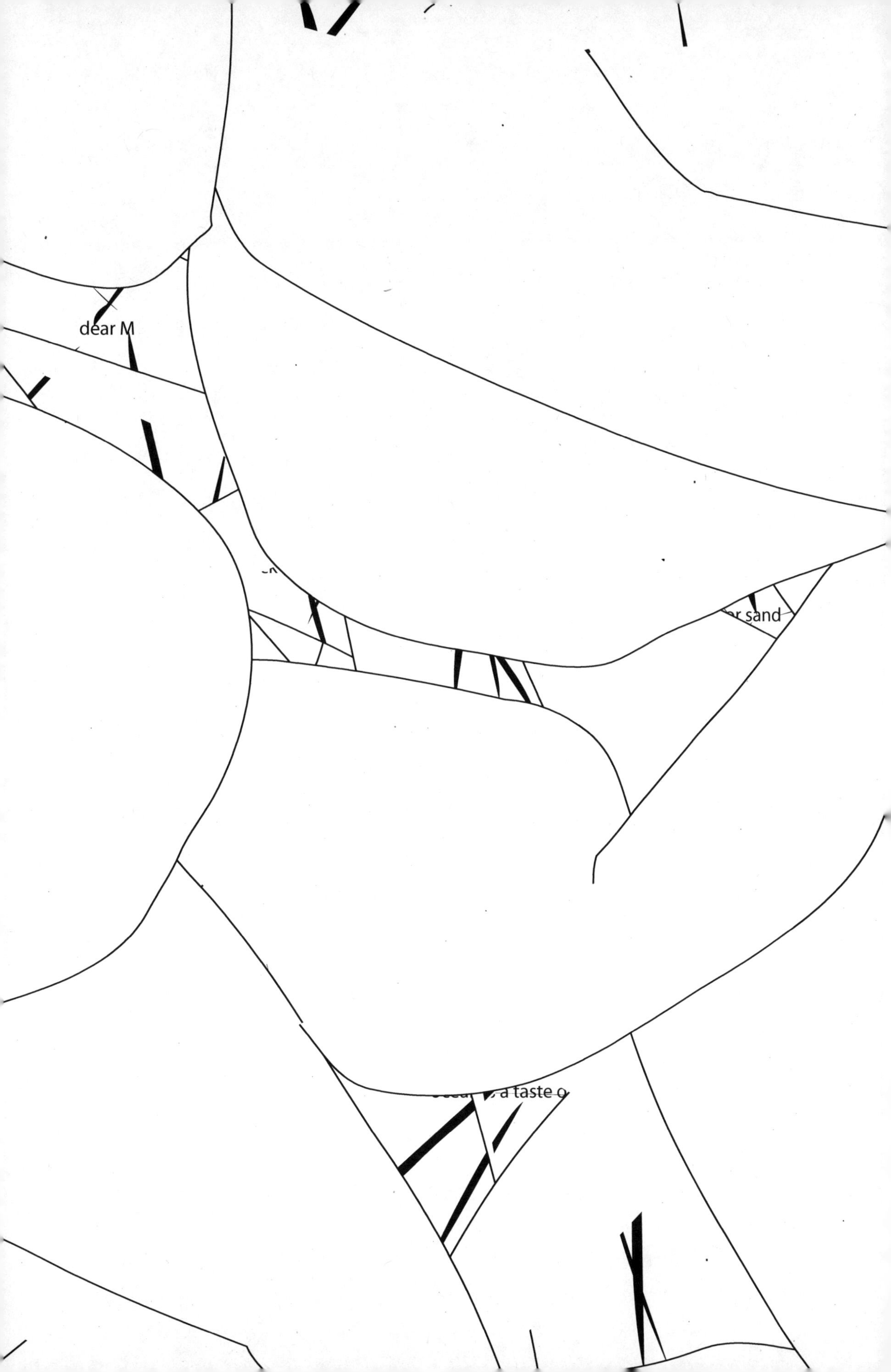

dear M
sand
a taste o

# HORIZON TALE

And if you lie flat
in a minute, is it because
you went unaware of the pre-
math, the stats, the
winged departure

*grow indigo hair flecked*
*with sea glass, becks*
*& twice-used bird wings*

## SHE, IN A TELEPHONE

speaks the lame affirmations,
renders the wires
in the declining sun
if the silence speaks louder.

flings the fennel into the champagne &
makes a dash for the stars

someone is laughing in close cotton

who knows what toxins would enter
if you gave radish rest,
rest you deserve to incline

*but they dodged the question: what is sadness?*

IN THE STAIRCASE
*is there nothing not contextual?*

(you make your life in the stairs
caught ruptured healing
catching recovering leaping)

speak listen give the 8-ball a turn
& reveal you you
one more chance

*as when you drop a book just now and the sound drops before it hits*

Should we gather & cluster around?

*And if this book could bruise a body, as an apple, what then?*

The person who was to fix
the passage of time is
a continuous no-show.

## MAN HOW TO LISTEN

*the horizon has an edge.*

It is a place & we live here,

under the grass, over the earth.

No pomegranate tree grows

under there, there where only

demons bring fruit.

*Listen, listen, listen list list list ist ist is is is i*

eight houses bulldozed

yet here, here

thickly it rings the bowl with the saliva edge. Mechoui is served: are you still nearby? Here in this place they kiss and so we know that life continues on apace. We traced the canyons with the wrinkles of our palms, I tell you this

SHE, COMES IN,
the charts go haywire

dangle the tail whether severed
or not, sing alphabets, sing Egyptian
nursery rhyme, sing mayhem,
sing sugar

*why must we only waste away at the horizon, can we not live there also?*

I washed an autumn leaf in the washing machine:
it looks remarkably like the leaf it was, no cleaner.
You cannot wash away death, & would you wish to,
it too is beautiful, if precisely because unknown.
It hits the living like a sword in the side ( I have
never felt a sword in the side, but I have felt the
nearness of the eye of death & it reflects much)

*we need a logician here. someone to explain*

Life you have come upon us like this, chosen us, with no explanation

SHE ON A LANDING

*for in that fragility is the strength*

FIRST PERSON PLURAL

Scene. Act (say six?) a character, as in father.

SHE IN A CHAIR
can you tell us how
to make rotten ticks
tock true?

*I wish to go forward in time.*

the words may be written far away from us (we just wait)
the world could have taken a turn here but it didn't,
we can't learn. a jelly fish came out and that's all,
the random recital of rain. this no performance
but an ongoing melody (you are underground: in this way
you do not have to own up to earth) it's round it keeps going
we lost the curve of the earth, door paper, adding up to sums.
the structure or gap is there. for the spiritual. we rise to enter it.

*In the vicinity, on the horizon, weathered but ambulatory, tenacious, she smiled at me*

SHE IN AN ELEVATOR
SHAFT, and in between the
floors, what is it that
you see?

an oddity, that raw
& dusty cement, why
are you stopped there
before it? who in that
air of landings?

SHE, IN THE CARS,

before the cars.
And if you lie flat
in a minute, is it because
you went unaware of the pre-
math, the stats, the
winged departure

What is the present but this thing that you are in?

(SHE, GO INTO THE CURVE)

I will go with you.

*The librarians of the soul are asked to come now.*

*Coda*

Who cut the umbilical cord on
words? Are we not animals first, we
sitting in conference rooms, repeating
anecdotes, drinking red wine
afterwards.
I have felt it, the absence of a tail. How
to listen when there is
all that. To touch.

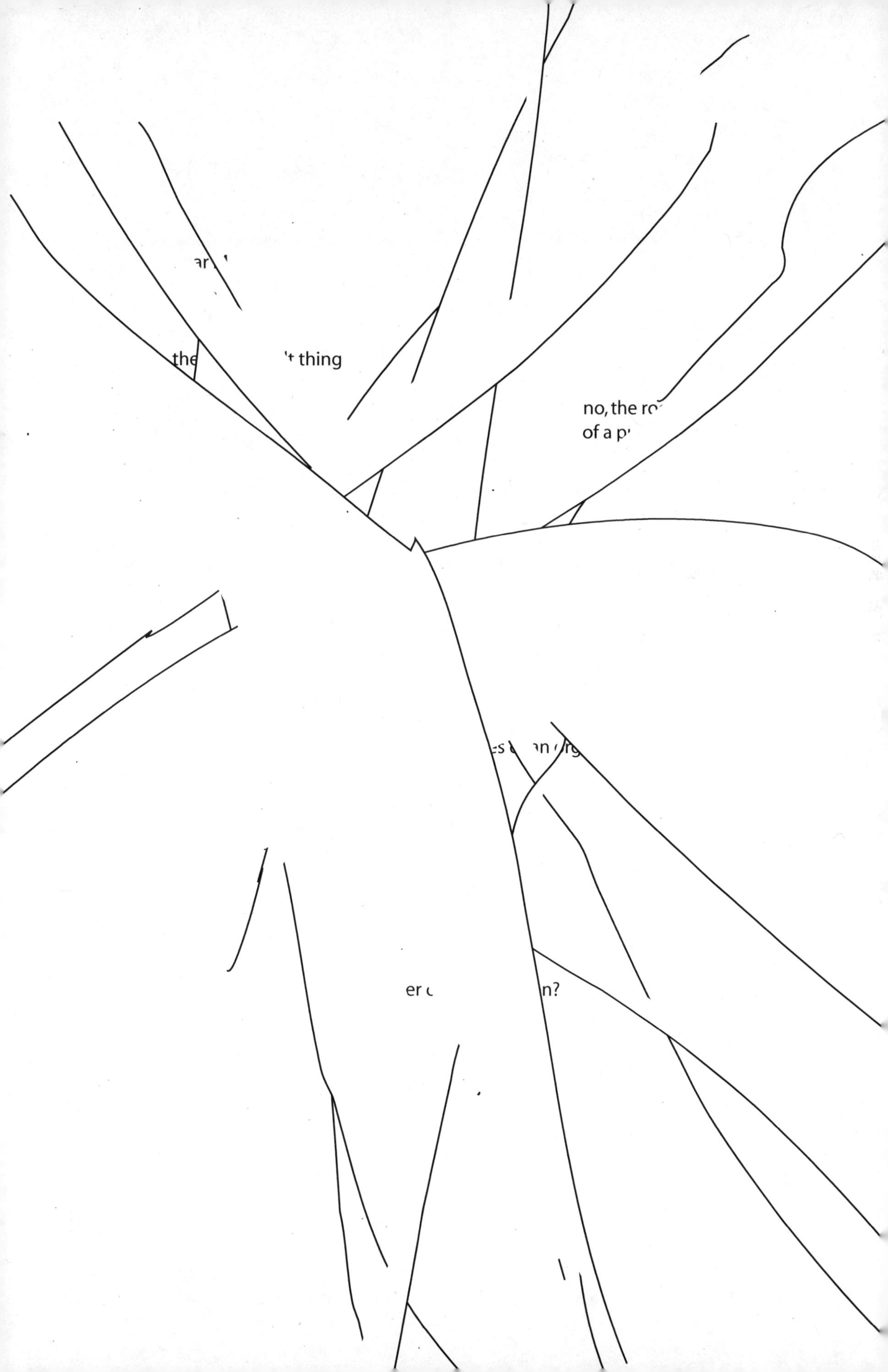
ar
the 't thing
no, the ro
of a p
es an org
er n?

# LETTERS TO THE DEAD

Dear D   h,

So it was you, not at the door, but inside my ear. This way you do not
need to knock. And while I can never be sure I hear you. Still there is this knowledge:
you are there. Already inside me, as sure as a baby inside preparing to get out. All the
instructions are inside.

All we ever had to do was to listen. When first we were together,
we were apart, and then there was the writing. We live through letters.
Though you never wrote to me, but to slam the door, as on a room full
of water. Some seepage under the door. Yet I not recognizing it there in the balcony
in the sun: it ends.

Dear Demeter,

For years I invited you for visits, it was not your fault. You looked in the drawers at the forks, it was the excitement. I came out of you and into the world but we grew up in a house of staircases, it only made sense that I would climb, both up and down.

The rendered panes cannot be further broken or displaced. We are down here and it is dark. It is the way of the world to be under itself even as it overdoes it.

We can't be together. I can't be saved. Nor you.

But there is spring: the hyacinth, the forsythia, the pansy, outside of 139 Pelleport. The spring is on its way in the form of a rabbit we saw in the metro entry at Bastille, eating lettuce on cardboard.

Dear Virginia,

I thought of you as I was getting out of the bath, not of a novel but of the years, how they fill or flatten, the happier we are the faster time goes. I thought of horizontality, the precision of illness, your need for space universalized to Kantian proportions, your fear of wards, of repetition, of the repetition of wars, nearby, of the poetry journal you nearly had, the children you wished to have—what would they have been like? and I think of the men, the servants, the lighthouse, the strength of Mrs. Dalloway and Ramsay, in all that flux, that hyperspeed of emotions, held by the stature, the static, the love, of a man, a husband, a degree of verticality in all that horizontality, that knowledge of the ill, the dying, the morose, the melancholic, the alcoholic, that intimate knowledge of the sky, the waves, water, waves.

I am glad you left a note for Leonard. I have found it many times in my mind, and I want you back. I don't know you at all. But I have plagiarized you till you've become me. The day I finished *To the Lighthouse* the fifth summer in a row, along a path of diminishing novel reading, we started to look for an actual lighthouse. To visit. To fill. To try. Good-bye Virginia. Those I have loved extremely well become part of me. And I have learned to feel what it is to swim.

Dear Will,

I discovered what it was I wanted to mention to you about islands, the cacophony of sounds, and the egos of books. It's this: I've named the applebook Will after you, he makes a twangling of sweet but strange sounds, and I will not give my heart to him, though being lightweight he will accompany me even on occasion to bed. The thing about islands and old age and books is that I've known them as elements of a sweet and generous past, fragile, and now partly gone.

I fell in love with one of you briefly, a vertigo of ironic brilliant head shots, smiling at me as if I too knew cobble lanes and lonely foraging kings and above all the devoted daughter who floats face-up. You entered me shortly, metaphorically, ye England with your corals and shackles and hawks. Damn, love sinks to the bottom and we in our bodies swim or glide on top. Let us swim.

Dear Christine,

We were in Carcassonne and it reminded me of the *City of Ladies*, so often I've fantasized of making buildings out of concrete blocks, starting from scratch, doing the work of the manual labourer, not this metaphorical work which pushes at concretion, is all the time calling, pulling, pleading at life.

There, you, constructing with a plume, laying the Pisan foundations, heavy-lifting with a forefinger and thumb. You are a sort of heroine of the independent, sitting in a room on your own, and creating as the philosopher would have it, not for yourself alone, but for all women. His clockwork, your decision. Precision city.

Dear Victor Noir,

What I want is the feather behind your ear if not the father in your wristwatch. I should like to make love to you in the here and now. To share the ecstasy. To enter you around your cock till you also are inside of me. But I have kissed you in the place between your breast pockets until feeling you cold as copper. Is it we women who have an excess to give, thinking your locks soft and your pants draping, hurtling our bodies upon a prone statue. You shall always remain twenty and something past, and we, where the fencing sword dropped, pregnant with other. Our child is the body of difference and same.

Dear Rain,

You enter into the earth, saturate it. Now comes from a country
of the sun, only before that married to hell, and then to Purgatory—
each time seven years. But I have made my way up, which is also a way of going
down. To reach the high notes, you have two mouths: one at the back of your neck
that opens out, and one which is your mouth, which is the front. It's like yawning,
which is near sleep, near.

Dear Snow,

Can I come into you now? It snowed in the inside of my body.

We are lofted now by a third, an energy between us.

Dear Cat (on a theme of holes)

*I heard in your hair how the wind pleats*

The range of sparkle diminishes here/there/here

These six letters of separation *reversed* in lovemaking

Where under this world is the one that makes us care for this one

Why, when the cloud removes itself and the words rise to take its place

Do you kiss me just now and with such complexity

dear M

the eye of blue is yellow

a wet line

the scent of s an eye

or sand

the c ulus of touch is red

i

the touch of sound i blue

cean is a taste of eye

S

With warm thanks to

Journals & Publications,

*American Letters & Commentary*

*The Denver Quarterly*

*Eponyme*

*The Nation*

*Phylogeny*

*10th Muse*

*Strangers in Paris: New Writing Inspired by the City of Light*

*Web Conjunctions*

Individuals,

Sarita Beraha, Omar Berrada, Safira Berrada Riggs, Oscarine Bosquet, Stéphane Bouquet, Vincent Broqua, Julia Carlson, Jeff Clark, Ben Doller, Sandra Doller, Stacy Doris, Megan Fernandes, Isabelle Garron, Peter Gizzi, Amy Harris, Emmelene Landon, Brenda Laws, Rachel Levitsky, Alberto Manguel, Michael Palmer, Doris Lessing, Marjorie Levinson, Sabine Macher, Stefania Pandolfo, Anna Rabinowitz, Bin Ramke, Srikanth Chicu Reddy, Wendy Riggs, Denise Riley, Joe Ross, Simona Schneider, Eleni Sikelianos, Meredith Spangler, Frederic Tcheng, Jennifer Vetter, Anne Waldman, Binky Walker, Marina Warner, Elizabeth Willis

dear M

the eye of blue is yellow

a wet line

the scent of s an eye

or sand

the c ulus of touch is red

i

the touch of sound i blue

cean is a taste of eye

S

*Pomme & Granite* is Sarah Riggs' fifth book of poetry in English, following *Waterwork* (Chax, 2007), *Chain of Minuscule Decisions in the Form of a Feeling* (Reality Street, 2007), *60 Textos* (Ugly Duckling Presse, 2010), and *Autobiography of Envelopes* (Burning Deck, 2012). She has published numerous collections in France, including *43 post-Its* and 28 télégrammes (Editions de l'Attente, 2006 & 2009), and the bi-lingual poem "Each dix minutes" (Contrat Maint, 2015). Her translations from contemporary French poetry into English include books by Marie Borel, Isabelle Garron, Ryoko Sekiguchi, and Oscarine Bosquet. Sarah Riggs' writing pushes into other forms, especially film, painting and dance. Her feature-length film, *Six Lives: A Cinepoem* (2014), plumbs the depths of understanding between film, the eye and the body through the work of Virginia Woolf (www.sarahriggs.org). Her paintings and drawings have been shown at galleries in Montreal and Paris, and her work in dance at spaces in Marrakech, Casablanca and New York through the collective Tamaas (www.tamaas.org) which she co-directs with writer and curator Omar Berrada. Riggs currently teaches at Pratt Institute.